Memento Vivere

Rachel BORTHWICK

BookLeaf Publishing

Presentation by *BookLeaf Publishing*

Web: www.bookleafpub.com

E-mail: info@bookleafpub.com

ISBN: 9789357445344

First edition 2021

DEDICATION

Dedicated to my Dad, Shuki and my children, Nicolas George and Fern Shuki. I love you.

October

Grubby fingerprints stained walls that had since
long forgotten,
And tired wooden beams soaked up squeals that
hadn't been heard for more than two decades.
Bannisters delighted at being gripped by chubby
fingers, needed for support again after all these
years.
And a man in his sixties knelt down to play with
a tiny boy who called him 'Poppy'.

It was a week in October:
A family swelled to five again and hearts
swelled, too.
Late mornings gave way to pre-dawn tiptoes
down the hallway,
A household up and fuelled by coffee.
A tiny boy fuelled by double the morning love
he was used to.

We did not know.
How could we?
That this would be the last October we would
ever feel like this.

Now the walls, the beams, the bannisters echo with the sounds of a man who was once called Poppy.

This Stubborn Man

His stubborn cough punctuated their nights.
An unwelcome interruption to the silence of
after-dark suburbia.
The days wore on and the hacking wore her
down.
Constant pleas to 'See the doctor' danced
mockingly in the Winter (and then Springtime)
air.
And then, finally a Tuesday morning witnessed a
yield.
This stubborn man, with his stubborn cough,
sought an answer to his question.

The Beginning

Monday afternoon, the Summer sun still high in
the sky.
I stand waiting on the corner, the beg button
slowly chirping, ready to give permission to
cross.
Suddenly, the shrillness competes with the
too-loud tones of a ringing phone.
It's mine.
It's Mum.
It's not like her to call.
And it is in that moment that I sharply inhale, I
know that this is the beginning.
Cancer.

The Baby

'Tell him first, lift him up.'
The news that we had a baby on the way.
As if it had the power to heal.
It almost did.
'You're going to be a grandfather. Again.'
A smile of disbelief came before a smile of
understanding.
'You haven't told your mother yet.'
A secret just for him, for a little while longer.

Twenty Three Years Ago

Twenty three years ago, I walked laps around
our pool.
Barefoot and barely caring if I overbalanced.

My toes caught every now and again in the
concrete that held together the sand-coloured
pavers.

Hours passed and as the light faded and my belly
grew hungrier,
I wandered back inside.
Inside to the whirring and groaning of the
machine.

He sat there,
Resigned to his part-time post while his blood
was washed of impurities.

And then.
The call.

So wanted but so seemingly out of reach.

A second chance, a third kidney and the first
taste of freedom in months.

Thank you for staying,
Just a little while longer.

The Last Photo

The beauty in the imperfections.
A chubby belly showing and a head shaved
ready for chemo.
The messy lounge they were perched upon.
One always camera-ready; the other squirming
to get free.
The last photo of a boy and his Poppy.

On the Eve of 35

On the eve of 35,
I only have one birthday wish.
Just a few minutes more with my Dad.

It will never be,
So I'll continue to look for him.

In the sky,
In my baby's dance moves,
And in the way my own eyes crinkle in the
corners.

This is the heaviest sadness,
My shoulders slump under the weight.

Every day becomes the longest time without
you,
But closer I inch to seeing you again.

You'll always be my birthday wish.

Proud From Paradise

I want the mundane,
The everyday.
The 'what's for dinner?'
Repeating the new word my son learned this
morning.
There's so much you're missing.
And I wonder:
Can you be proud from paradise?

The World

You were there with me this morning, at 2am.
While the rest of the world lay still.
I heard you in the echo of the waves,
Bouncing off my lounge room walls.
In the same places where the sunlight usually
hits.

I look for you in the slow moments,
When little hands aren't grappling for mine.
When the background noises finally cease.
I don't know how else to do this.
I don't know how else to live this life,
To love this life,
That you're no longer in.

I mark the passage of time by Thursdays.
It's the day you went away.
Four Thursdays of monotony and routine
snaking it's way back in through the cracks.
While the rest of the world marches on.

You were only here but a moment ago,
Still I fear the colours will fade and I won't
know how to keep up.
I have become unstitched,

The thread pulling away from me the harder I
hold on.
Every day I sit and wait,
Although for what?
I'm not entirely sure.

I'm winded each time I see your image,
Moments captured in time that will never return.
My eyes sting and I swallow away the fire in my
throat.
Then, I look around at the rest of the world and I
know.

To us, you are the world.

A World of Contrasts

Time is measured by the life growing inside of
me,
And the life that was extinguished before me.

I'm the daughter who idolised you,
Yet my daughter will never know you.

They tell me you're always with me,
But where? I need you here.

Only once have you come to me in my dreams.
You said I would be alright.
I'm not.

I am not.

A world of contrasts.

Your death has rearranged my world.

Where does all the love go when there is
nowhere to put it?

Roast Beef

The roast beef sat untouched,
The early hours of Christmas morning.

Sleep would never come;
We tried anyway.

The rhythm of the night forever different,
A gaping hole, so much more than human-sized.

The baby slept through,
Never knowing the hours we had spent saying
goodbye.

The sun rose despite our protestations.
A broken family who could never bring
themselves to eat the roast beef.

Home

Bananas sit in someone else's fruit bowl now.
The cereal is nearly out of date.

There's an indent in the lounge,
In the very place you used to sit.

Someone else stokes the fire now,
Winter feels that much bitter.

One less toothbrush spatters the mirror,
An empty towel rail begs to be warmed.

Home.
It's where your heart was.

The Fever

The days collide.
Unrivalled.
Bar for far-flung foreign streets.

Sunlight snatched in greedy moments.
We pounce, as it wakes and then steadies for
imminent slumber.

Our little one knows nothing of all of this,
A fractured normal,
Now this is his norm.

One day, he'll ask why the photos paused,
Of toes crusted with sand grains,
Of beach towels clutched by chubby hands.

The skies are quiet,
Yet upwards he still gazes.
Searching for the roar of engines that would
punctuate the day.

But then.

The silence fades into a rhythmic knock.

At the door, our neighbour hands me a white
paper bag.

Inside,
A technicoloured toy.
An egg,
For now it is Easter.

An impatient fist of foam finds its way into my
baby's mouth.
He squeals,
Feverishly.

It was a fever that began this,
And joyously,
There will be a fever when it ends.

The Arrival

Two months with her.

Eyelashes curl upwards and tickle her skin,
Black and thick like mine.

Suddenly, she's five.

Her fingers dance clumsily on ivory keys,
Toes scraping the ground as they swing back and
forth.

Ten and bold.

Her limbs are long and lithe,
I greedily hold her arms around me just a
moment more.

Fifteen years old.

Her eyes are deep clear pools,
They're wide and wild.

Fern,
One day we'll be able to share you with the
world.

The Welcome Ghost

Guilt as intoxicating as shame,
You've been absent from my thoughts for hours.

Out of sight, out of mind.
The cruellest reality.

How will I live life without you?
And then I realise that I already am.

And then I'm caught off guard,
Stumbling over my thoughts.

You'll be there,
In my mind the way you ought to be.

Distractions take over,
Whether I invite them or not.

Just know,
You'll always be my welcome ghost.

In Two

If I could see inside myself, I'm sure I'd be split in two.

The me who had a father.

And the me who doesn't.

I don't know myself yet. This new version of someone I had grown to love.

I'm quick to anger now, and slow to forgive.

I don't recognise myself yet. This new version of someone so predictable.

I'm short-tempered now, and long in the face.

I don't like myself yet. This new version of someone who has changed so immeasurably.

If I could see inside myself, I'm sure I'd be split in two.

Limbo

I'm being suspended,
But cannot see the strings.

A life in limbo,
Teetering on the edge.

Nothingness,
How do I go where you are?

Where do you rest?
The uncertainty engulfs me.

'If we choose the plaque,
Then it will feel real.'

Then let's just wait,
A little bit longer.

The Passionfruit Vine

You pass a spoonful of the honey-coloured pulp,
There's a bitter crunch of seeds and a
lip-puckering tang.

Blades of grass cling to your ankles in
desperation;
The fade to brown and lifeless inevitable.

Liquid fizzes and spits,
And triangular cubes of ice struggle to compete
with the sun's ferocity.

A rapidly-moving bead of sweat drips into your
eye,
And you squint.

The motor of the lawnmower comes to an
eventual stop,
Silence stands no chance as the chants of cicadas
swiftly take over.

The trampoline,

Rusted and lonely.

Waits for tanned Summer limbs to bounce once
again,
Framed in colour by the passionfruit vine.